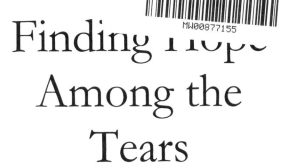

Finding Hope Among the Tears

Linda Vickery St Myers

"They who sow in tears shall
reap in joy and singing."
Psalm 126:5

ISBN: 1483912906
ISBN-13: 9781483912905

Dedicated

to

everyone who's

LIFE

has been

SHATTERED

from

DIVORCE

and

SURVIVED

to find

HOPE

for a New Life!

Linda St. Myers is touching women who are hurting and struggling in their everyday lives, by helping women to empower themselves into finding true happiness and embracing the now. She attended Life Purpose Institute to be certified as a Life Purpose and Spiritual Coach to enhance her ministry "Patchwork Ministry". She believes that putting the pieces of our lives back together again we all can become God's beautiful quilt. Linda lives in Cincinnati, Ohio and has 2 beautiful daughters, Stephanie and Sara, fabulous sons-in-law Kevin and Justin, step-daughter Robin, and is the proud Grandma of Alex, Joshua, Colin, Zachary and Taylor.

Table of Contents

"The most painful tears are not the ones

that fall from my eyes

and cover my face,

It is the ones that fall from my heart

and cover my soul."

~Author Unknown

~ *Prologue* ~

It was November 5th 2003 when my life as I knew it came to an end, the end of my 34 year marriage.

GOD WILL GIVE YOU THE VISION AND IT IS UP TO YOU TO BRING IT TO LIFE. God revealed to me to write my story and I asked, "Why Mine?" So it began the summer of 2006 on my trip to California to study to become a "Life Coach" and find my life's purpose after a devastating divorce in 2004. God started working on me when I stepped on that plane and he hasn't stopped yet and I know he won't! I am definitely a work in progress as God shows me what to do with my life. HOW TO HELP OTHERS!

He showed me this vision to write 6 Simple Read books that will help others to learn to step out of their comfort box and cope with life's unwelcomed adversities. So this is the beginning of my vision and how God has carried me and finally put me down to walk beside HIM hand in hand, hour-by-hour, day-by-day, and month-by-month. At times it came down to God helping me minute by minute of each day. Only God can see us through our ups and downs, around and over, and turn darkness into light, and I praise him for my survival to tell you my story of HOPE, HAPPINESS, FORGIVENESS and PATIENCE knowing these are truly gifts from GOD.

So, after 10 years of healing and getting my life in order and embracing the NOW it is time to release my words, my story, to help others know they can heal through the loving arms of our Savior, Jesus Christ.

"Be strong, courageous, and firm;
Fear not nor be in terror before them,
For it is the Lord your God who goes with you;
He will not fail you or forsake you."
Deuteronomy 31:6 Amplified

~ Forward ~

To me, a true friend is someone who stands by you when you are down and celebrates with you when you are up. It is someone you trust, someone who understands you, knows the real you and appreciates the person you are. That is who Linda is to me.

I met Linda while working. She sold radio advertising for a local radio station and I was marketing and public relations for a local company. Therefore, we would meet to talk about advertising. It wasn't long that we found we had similar interests. We were both divorced. We shared our stories. The difference was she had just experienced the horrible betrayal both from her husband and her best friend. My heart ached for her. We became instant friends. As time went on, Linda mentioned that she wanted to help women going through life's struggles that changes their way of living. She did not want anyone to feel the isolation she felt during this terrifying time. So, she boarded a plane and headed to California to become a Life Coach. WOW! What a way to turn a negative situation into a positive! Through this she also was able to reconnect with God, whom she felt during her marriage she had to put "on the back burner."

She was able to put the past behind her for a time to really get to know herself, what she wanted and where she wanted to be. Moving from a small rural area of

Greenville, Ohio to a much bigger city of Cincinnati was just what she needed. We would spend hours on the phone at night talking about the pain and the growth of her situation. I witnessed her emotions of fear, pain, mistrust, dependency, low self-esteem, anger, resentment and many other negative feelings before she became happy, content, satisfied and joyful about her life again! And she did this with her true friend, me and most importantly, her relationship with God.

This book is filled with real life "stuff." The stuff that so many of us have experienced, with or without friends, divorced or married. Linda expresses herself by writing about her toughest battles, emotionally and physically. She also tells how she turned herself around with the grace of God on her side. With God all things are possible and with each chapter Linda shows her readers just that. The peace and love she has found in her life through Christ is amazing. When God brings you to it, he will bring you through it.

When she asked me to write this foreword for her I was honored. God has showed me how to be a true friend and in showing me that he gave me a true friend back.

Blessing Linda…you deserve it!

~Tasha Anderson

"Someday" You Said

When do they end?
Those tears from a struggling heart.
When can I say "I feel no pain"?
The pain from a struggling heart.
When do the pieces of my broken heart heal?
The pieces of a struggling heart.

"Someday" you said Lord, "Patience" my child.
"Your day will come, in my time, not yours."
You must shed those tears.
You must feel the pain.
The heart must break, you'll see someday.

The day has come,
When the tears have stopped.
The day has come,
When the pain has left.
The day has come,
When the pieces feel whole.
You did say "Someday".

You were right, Lord.
You gave me the patience,
To see me through.
You held me tight,
In those long dark days.
You held my hand,
And led me to the light.
Thank you LORD,
For healing my struggling heart.
~Linda St Myers
March 17, 2011

Chapter 1

From the Beginning........

All is Well in My Life, so I thought.......

Have you felt your life is going along fine and you have it all together? You raised your children through high school, college, one wedding, and another one coming up. Now it is time for you and your spouse to finish out your lives **"together"** in peace and harmony by discovering new things to do **"together"**.

You're living a comfortable life, have a beautiful home, a vacation home on the lake, boat, and driving nice cars. You have started talking about retirement and a possible home in Florida **"together"**. You are looking forward to celebrating your 40th and anticipating your 50th **"together"**. Your children have begun their lives gracing you with grandchildren so you can spoil and cherish every moment with them **"together"**. My life **"together"** was in order, so I thought....

Of course I had my share of trial and tribulations from childhood through those tough teenage years right into my adulthood to this time of my midlife. I was looking forward to my senior years "**together**". All our lives have a beginning no matter when that beginning comes…today, tomorrow, or the day you were born, but I choose to begin from the beginning.

When all of a sudden out of the blue a bolt of lightning struck me in the center of my heart…..literally. The world that I knew came crushing down around me. My dreams gone, shattered into pieces like a jigsaw puzzle unable to put them together again.

The life I knew was taken away, for he wanted out, telling me he no longer "loved me". Over, just like that, no warning, no trying to work it out. That lightning bolt severed my heart and zapped all my strength to live. I was unable to pick up the puzzle pieces piled in front of me to make them into a beautiful picture called "Life". Nothing matched, and they sure did not fit.

What do I do now? Where do I go? I was not prepared. No one is. No one to turn to –**all alone**- the "**together**" now "**one**", "**single**" and learning how to piece together my puzzle by taking one piece at a time and trying every which way I could to make it fit.

"I knew you before I formed you in your

Mother's womb. Before you were born I

set you apart and appointed you as spokesman

to the world."

Jeremiah 1:5 NIV

God was an important part of my life as I was growing up. My parents were very loving Christians who knew the value of living a Christ-centered life. As children we did all the fun things, but most importantly, they did not let us wander away from the church during our teenage years. They supported me in all my adventures at church. The day came when I accepted Jesus as my Lord and Savior at a church work camp at the College of the Ozarks in Arkansas in 1966. I knew I wanted to be a follower of Jesus Christ and to help other teenagers find a path to God.

My church was everything to me because it was my safe place-where others my age accepted me for who I was. We did not have the pressures the kids experience today 'back in the good old days' of the fifties and sixties. Family values where esteemed and we respected our elders. But growing up did have some of those ups and downs. I was the little girl no one wanted to play with or on their team unless they had to pick me. I wasn't good enough. I don't remember how many times I packed a bag just to run away.

I suffered almost daily with severe earaches until I was in 3rd grade. I went through radiation treatments and finally surgery to remove built-up scar tissue. I can remember sitting in class at school with a towel leaning against the radiators just to make it through the day. My dad and my uncle would blow smoke in my ears for the warmth to ease the pain. I remember crying with them and then within days I would suffer from leg aches at night. I don't think we ever found out the correlation between the two, but I can tell you I remember the pain and crying out to my parents to get me some relief.

During my childhood my only wish was to have my own horse. That day came when my dad and a family friend bought several ponies at an auction. I not only had one but several. Our two families spent hours riding and my sanctuary became the barn. We soon outgrew the ponies and went in the horse business. My first horse was a 17 hands tall perfect golden palomino.

In high school, I worked every day after school and on Saturdays (we were not open on Sunday, remember those days) so school activities were limited along with friends. They came and went. I never fit in with any certain group. My best friend became my Palomino horse named "Sinbad's Golden Clipper". He was the Great Grandson of the Palomino Arthur Godfrey would ride in the Rose Bowl Parade. Clipper and I would ride for hours, alone in God's world.

I am sure many of you have been in this situation. So I found my life working at my Uncle's 5 & 10 in the record department spinning records, riding Clipper, and being at church. I attended Sunday School, sang in the choirs, youth fellowship, church camps every year, and I made God the center of my life.

God wants to use us for **HIS** purpose, to go out into the world and shout about His greatness; to tell the world what He has done for us… changing our lives and how to live a life fulfilled. I lost control of who I was and what my life purpose was to be when my "togetherness" became one.

Chapter 2

For Better or Worse.......

Then one day another person came into my life. His name was Pat and we were married on February 22, 1969. I kidded around that I made him get married on Washington's Birthday so he couldn't tell a lie but little did I know our marriage would become full of lies and deceit. We were happy newlyweds as everyone is in the beginning. We had fun....many friends....many parties. But soon I came to realize God and church was not going to be part of our "**togetherness**". So, the first years of our marriage, I drifted in and out of church.... always by myself, until I walked away completely.

With 4 years of fun "**together**" we talked about having children but nothing was happening. After several serious operations and fertility pills our first daughter Stephanie was born on August 10, 1973, and put into my arms to be loved and cared for. First thing I said was, "She looked like her dad". I was thankful to God for giving me such a beautiful baby girl, we named her Stephanie. When the doctors were not sure I would ever have any children.

So now what do I do? A new mother, with a beautiful little girl to raise…..God in my heart, but unable to have a relationship with Him. Even though we had her baptized, as a family we could not make a commitment to have the Lord and church a part of our lives.

On July 14, 1976, I was facing the birth of our 2nd daughter, complications during delivery was taking my life away. With a room full of student nurses eagerly watching, I was in trouble. The birth of Sara was over, but all of a sudden I was hearing the doctors and nurses shouting out orders, "emergency hysterectomy", "get her out", "get her under", "she is going into shock". I remember the pain-oh, so painful, more than the delivery itself. A nurse was whispering in my ear to relax my body. I was retching in pain, and it was so difficult to relax. My life was flashing in front of me and I was slipping away. What was going to happen? My uterus prolapsed, turned inside out coming out, and was with the placenta. I was screaming in pain, but I was also screaming out to God, "He cannot raise these girls by himself – please help me."

I was hoping God would help someone who had not been at all faithful to him, someone who abandoned him....**WAS I TOO LATE**? But God heard my cries to save my life. They said the next 24 hours would be crucial and if I made to morning I would be okay. When I was finally aware of what had happened I realized there were two lines inserted on each side of my neck forcing fluid and blood. I could not move a muscle because I had strained every single one in my body. The kind nurses had to roll me side to side for days. I was spared, and when they put Sara into my arms I knew there would always be a special bond between us, which carries today. He gave me my life back to watch my 2 daughters, Stephanie and Sara, grow to be beautiful loving women and mothers with families of their own.

But this did not convince me to go fully back into God's fold. It changed me to the point I knew I could not live without God in my life. I knew I needed an open relationship with him but it wasn't going to happen. Instead I became a closet Christian silently praying alone.

I was not yet listening to Him fully, and I had failed God's plan for my life... I failed to set priorities. I had failed to be disciplined in a day to day life with Christ. I failed to tell others about God's unconditional love and I failed to step up to the plate and say thank you for sparing my life. I failed.....

Sara was also baptized within a couple years of her birth, but as a family I still could not get the commitment I wanted to attend church regularly as a family. So I took the girls alone, sent them to Sunday school, and even taught Sunday school, but as time went along and the girls got older we drifted away again.

I prayed quietly in my own little closet but I was not asking for the right things. I was asking God to come into our marriage and help me deal with another problem. I was living with someone who had become an everyday drinker. You see I became a victim to alcoholism. I attended al-a-non for five years trying to find answers to why and how I could save my husband. I got us into debt several times to support the girls and our family needs. I couldn't write a check for groceries or clothes and I became good at robbing Peter to pay Paul or borrowing without his knowledge until it would catch up with me. I knew this was wrong, but it came down to survival of my family.

Still praying in the closet the answers were not coming. Lying became easier because arguments with someone who drinks never turn out well. I was living on eggshells. I learned when I could have a decent conversation with him and when it was time to just be quiet. I was screaming for help from anyone who would listen-friends, family members, anyone. No one was there. Not even God, I thought. I prayed but I did not think my prayers were being answered.

My husband constantly told me he was the king and I was his pawn. He accused me of having affairs whenever I left the house. I was living a life of verbal abuse, but fortunately no physical abuse. There are times when verbal abuse can be worse than physical because bruises go away and words are not easily forgotten. But when you hide so much, what kind of life was I living? It was wrong, and I take full responsibility for my deception, but at the time survival was more important.

It would have been easier to walk away and split up the family. Become a divorced single mom raising two girls, but I chose to stay in the marriage and make the best of it. I valued my marriage and the vows to God.

I continually thought I could change him. I valued family life, but now I wonder did I do the right thing. I might have cheated myself of a full and happy life filled with respect and love. I to this day believe he loved me the best way he could. Instead, our marriage became "a way of life" for me.

I bought a small advertising business from a relative and was told it had small liabilities, but it turned out to be $45,000 in debt. With no support from anyone I tried my best to bring it back. I bounced checks, borrowed just to keep from telling him the truth of just how bad it really was. When the truth came out and I closed the business we had 27 State Tax liens against our home not counting the numerous collectors constantly calling. I negotiated settlements and releases to keep from going to court. But for 10 years I heard every day that it was my fault, and we would not be in this credit mess if it wasn't for me. He hated my family for doing this to "him". I hated that it happened, but I could not change it. I began living the

"Serenity Prayer" every day. I had to continue to move ahead and put this behind me. He, however, could not.

All I tried to do was love him the best way I knew how. Reality was not a part of our lives. I did not like the person I had become with all the lies and deception and the games I played to keep everything looking normal. When the truth finally came out, as it always does, it didn't take long to go back. I just wanted the accusations to stop so I could stop. I just didn't want to hear about it from him. There wasn't a chance for an open and honest relationship between either of us. Our home became nothing but secrets and lies on my part. Life goes on, however, and whatever has to be done is done for the sake of peace. It became survival in the relationship of what I thought was **"togetherness"**.

Our lives took another change in 1991 when a call came into our home and a woman asked "Are you my Dad? My name is Robin." She was 26 and was told her father was not who she thought he was. "Yes I am"…were the words that came out of his mouth. I knew about her from the time we were married, but he never wanted to find her. She had a new life and her mother had chosen not to make him part of hers and Pat did not want to upset her life either. In the months prior to this call I felt the time was coming that she would appear.

She came to meet him on August 10th, 1991, and to this day

I have always wondered how she drove up to our home and walked to our door. I welcomed her into our family with open arms for she deserved to know who her Father was. Many people told me not get involved with her, but I could not do that. At times it was difficult for Stephanie and Sara, but today they are sisters.

She has never been my step-daughter because she was 26 when she came into my life.. She did not need a mother, but I told her I would be her friend. She has since completed nursing school with a lot of encouragement from me. I am so proud of her and the life she has created for herself and her daughter. I was able to attend her graduation and sat with her family and watched her receive her diploma. Knowing the struggles she had overcome herself. She is now a daughter I love. I do not get to see her as much as I would like, but I love her just the same.

Life went on with the girls' high school and college graduations, the wedding of Stephanie, my firstborn, and I welcomed a new son-in-law and a new step-daughter into my family.

All is well on the surface so it seemed……

Chapter 3

Spiraling Out of Control

By this time we seemed to be living a comfortable lifestyle with a beautiful home, swimming pool, a vacation home at Lake Erie, and we were talking about retirement. When POW…..my life came tumbling down around me. I was left holding onto just a piece of the twine, not a rope. Remember the vision of a frayed rope that has a single piece spinning around and around so fast? This is how I felt? That was me and it was sucking the life right out of me. I only had that single piece of twine to hold onto. The final spiral began during the year of 2002.

A chain of events, one after another, had control over me. It all started when I was named in a multi-million dollar lawsuit with a previous employer. I was overwhelmed by just the thought of going to court. I found out undercover detectives tape-recorded my conversations twice. Attorney's questioned me about what I said over a year prior.

I spent long days in depositions with attorney after attorney hammering at me about this and that. They put me under a microscope of ethics on how my working relationships with people were. Or they would shuffle me off to a room by myself pacing while they talked it out. This was my life passion-working with people helping them design the home of their dreams. Now it was looking as if my passion of new home sales was all going down the tube and out the window. The very career I loved so much.

I am sure you can agree that you could not remember what you did or said a year ago, let alone a week ago or seven sometimes a day or minute ago? Getting older does mean losing some of our memory. Under this kind of pressure you cannot do it and you're afraid of saying the wrong thing that would nail you to the wall. Luckily my story was found truthful and the events that occurred were not of my doing. I was soon released and the feeling of relief was getting back to normal or what I thought was normal. But that was not going to happen. Little did I know when I was taking things out of my name for protection, it would hurt me later in the divorce.

Remember, I was a closet non-committed Christian and not a good child of God yet. I did not ask for His help inside or out loud for that was not a priority in my life. You are supposed to turn to God for help through adversity. I was bouncing along in life without His help. Why start now? I could handle anything. Why go to God?

Without God the spiral continued, only speeding up

faster, faster, and faster. The lawsuit was coming to an end, but things began heating up in another situation with one of our closest friends.

Remember the game telephone we all played as kids where you tell the first person next to you something and by the time it gets around to the last person it can be completely different or at least a different meaning than when it began?

How many times in our lives as adults has this happened when we were talking with others and it got back to us so different than what we initially said?

This exact thing took place with a group of ladies with an organization I was president of, and it got so nasty in what was said and the actions that took place over several months, that it ended the friendship with our best friends of over 25 years as well as the emotional toll of losing lifetime friends was creeping into other areas of my life.

But what is done is done and the treasured memories will live on of camping, playing cards, Lake Erie and sharing our families with laughter and love that sadly came to an end because someone felt they needed to change the story. A friendship of over 25 years gone, but not forgotten with friends that cannot and will not be replaced. Note: We have started to communicate now, but I will never have that close friendship back again.

This was another devastating blow to me and it took a major toll on me mentally and physically as one adversity after another continued to suck the life from me. I was done. I had never experienced anything like it. I could describe it in one word..."hell"! I began questioning myself "what was going on? Was it ever going to end? What was going to happen next?" I needed to run but where was I going to go? Pat continued to blame me for everything. Nothing was his fault, and I never felt any support from him. I was alone to figure it all out for myself, never stopping to get on my knees and pray.

Well, that day came for the next shoe to fall. During the next three months, after the devastating loss of my friendship; my work was suffering in new home sales with another good friend and his family, he felt I could not do my job anymore and he let me go in July 2003 stating many reasons. These were friends we went on vacations with, and ate out with on a weekly a basis. This friendship was also coming to an end. What was happening? Is this ever going to end? I was spinning on that single twine so fast now I could not even stand up or stop. My life was out of control.

I knew it was hurting my relationship with Pat. What was I going to do? How could I change what had happened? It was done-over. He continued to blame me for everything that was going on in our lives. No support, only put downs and blame, everything was about what it was doing to him, not about what I was going through. Why could he not see my hurt, and my pain? Why could he not comfort me? But what did I expect? He was never there for me in the past, so why would he be now? Why was it about him?

"Try God"....not yet, I was still holding on to that last piece of twine with all my might. I could weather the storms of life. I had been doing it for 34 years but I was quickly slipping off the final strand. What was happening to me? I was still not asking the one I needed to....ASK GOD!!!! At this time he was still not a part of my life completely. Yet I knew deep down inside, from my teenage years, I should have known He was the one to deliver me from all this drama.

Lifetime friends GONE....job GONE....then on November 5, 2003, when I was 53 years old...married 34 years 8 months and 14 days, Pat told me he wanted a divorce. This was only 10 days before our daughter was to get married. With no possible reconciliation he had already made up his mind. He had seen an attorney and was not going to change his mind. He would be leaving me on Sunday after the wedding.

That same week the doctor found a lump in my breast. POW! AGAIN…I'm down and that spiraling twine I was hanging on to, well it just snapped! Darkness overtook me and the next days were a total blur. I went through the daily tasks of getting ready for the wedding, but I do not remember much of anything to this day. I can't go on. There is nothing left. I was done, broken and crying my eyes out.

I went to the pastor to talk to him about what was going on seeking comfort. Trying to find out why Pat picked this time to announce it.

Who should I tell, who should I not? Where do I go from here? My girls would be gone, I had no job. My health was not good.

The questions did not stop. He was done with me, and now I knew I needed to seek God's loving arms, but why would He be there for me? I left Him.

"The LORD is close to the brokenhearted;

He rescues those whose spirits are crushed."

Psalm 34:18 NLT

On Wednesday or Thursday I don't remember what day because shock had set in I was talking with my daughter Stephanie on the phone while working on bows with my best friend when I broke down and tried to tell her what was going on. I had to hand the phone to her and she finished telling her that her Dad would be leaving me on Sunday. She gave me a guardian angel to help me cope with everything while we were waiting on the results from the doctor. He was to let me know on this day.

The rehearsal and wedding day arrived for Sara and Justin. I was still in a blur of what had happened over the past ten days. I was trying to stay focused and not let my emotions show. But it was very difficult. I was exhausted, dazed and confused. Trying to keep my head held high for family and friends who came. I had not told anyone except the pastor, and now Stephanie and my immediate family. I asked that we not tell Sara and Justin until after their honeymoon but I found out much later that Pat told her at the rehearsal party. I can tell you if I had known this on that night, I would not be here to tell you my story.

Sitting alone and trying not to cry at the reception, exhausted, and heartbroken, words cannot describe the pain I was experiencing. Everyone was asking if I was okay, but I just made one excuse after another that I was tired. I was just going through the motions of what I needed to do as the mother of the bride. For someone who loves to dance I just could not drag myself out on the dance floor and it was apparent that Pat did not want anything to do with me either. When we did the parents dance you could just feel the tenseness between us. He didn't want to dance with me and I didn't want to dance with him. Why should he because he was leaving me the next day?

Even Sara and Justin came up to me at one time to get me to dance but I just could not. I did know they knew what was going on. I was numb and to this day I do not remember very much of that day and I still have trouble looking at any of the pictures.

Sunday morning came and everyone met at our home to open the gifts. Justin's family came too. When they got finished and we loaded everything into their cars for them to go back to Cincinnati we hugged and all I could think about was "please do not leave." I didn't want to be alone. My day would go downhill from here. Pat was leaving me.

Could things get any worse?

Monday morning came and I figured out he was leaving me for my best friend. The one who was helping me with the wedding and the one I had been there for during 2 of her divorces and the death of her fiancé just the year prior. She had called me to tell me she wasn't following him around at the reception even though I told her it was noticed by several and it was on video. Another friend of 25 years GONE, only this time gone with my husband.

She had become a third party in my marriage. I thought I was helping her, but instead she was opening herself up to accept Pat into her life. She said she tried to close the door to him but he kept coming back. She just didn't close the door hard enough. I should have seen the signs but why would I question my best friend on her intentions? Or Pat's either? I was oblivious because I was trying to overcome losing other lifetime friends, as well as my job, and I was busy planning a wedding. I was not focused on what they were doing. I thought we were helping her out as friends during her mourning. We took her to Lake Erie to fish, out to eat, planted a garden at her home, helping her out with her little mini farm. Sure makes me wonder how hard she really tried. Only she can answer that and someday she will, not to me, but to God.

I began to believe I was at fault for everything that

was happening. It was all catching up with me -- the lies, the deceit, the continued belittling that everything was always my fault. It was coming true. Everything he was saying to me and about me. I was this horrible person and I did it to him. I started to believe God was punishing me for all my mistakes. Living in the real world was too difficult, and it was easier to accept what people were saying about me. Everything was true. I could not stand up for myself. Instead, I let it all happen without fighting. There was no fight left.

The long days and nights ahead are still a blur, but I remember following him to her house and what pain that was putting me in. I just wanted to confront her, lash out, and scream. Ask her why she opened the door to him when I had been there for her so many times during her life struggles. Why? Why? Why? was all I could say.

One night, at one o'clock in the morning, I decided to drive over and take pictures of his car in her driveway. I was crying so hard I could not see the road. I took the pictures and on my way back home driving at a high rate of speed I had decided to end it all. I would just let go of the wheel and let the car go off the road and end my pain. She had my life, she had him – what did I have to look forward to?

All of a sudden there appeared a car heading towards me with brighter than normal headlights. The lights brought me back to my senses and I was able to stop at the stop sign. And guess what? It was a county sheriff. As I passed him, I stopped reversed my car, and talked to him. He settled me down after listening to me screaming and crying my heart out. He told me I was doing about 90 miles per hour coming toward him and if I hadn't stopped he would have turned around and given me a ticket. Instead he listened, and made sure I was capable of making it the rest of the way home. He was a guardian angel on a dark country road that night sent by God to keep me from ending my life. I never found out his name to thank him for saving my life, but God knows.

"We are pressed on every side by troubles,
but not crushed and broken.

We are perplexed because we don't know
why things happen as they do,

But we don't give up and quit.

We are hunted down,
But God never abandons us.

We get knocked down,
But we get up again and keep going.

These bodies of ours are constantly
Facing death just as Jesus did;

So clear to all that is only the living
Christ within (who keeps us safe).

2 Corinthians 8-10 NLV

I didn't see the signs and I sure didn't know how to listen, but God heard me screaming inside and began working in my life. God didn't give up on me and He won't give up on you.

"I can do everything through Him

Who gives me strength."

Philippians 4:13 NIV

Chapter 4

Under the Covers with my Feet Hanging out

I dedicate this chapter to those who have

buried their heads to keep from facing life.

That is exactly what I did. I buried myself from life for better than a year. I buried myself so deep in the tunnel I was living in, and it was so dark there was not even a speck of light that I could see. I was buried alive seeing no hope, no future, and had absolutely no energy to even try. The tears flowed day in and day out well into the night until there were no more to cry. The next day it just started over again.

My only position was curled up in a ball so tight either under the covers in bed or under covers on the couch with my feet hanging out. I cannot stand to have anything on my feet so when I am in bed my feet are always hanging out. If I didn't have to move I didn't. I was trying to find comfort within myself and it just was not there. And I did not like myself very well. Guilt and blame set in. When I tried to get up and function I found that I had became addicted to the prescription drugs they had given me, addicted to computer cards well into the night, addicted to the sound of my TV going 24/7. All of this just to try and hide the pain. None of it worked, and I would continue to ask those unanswered questions… "Why?"   "Why?" " Why?" " Was it ever going to end?"

The thoughts of suicide continued, crying out for help, yet no one there. I just wanted to fall asleep and not wake up to this nightmare. I did try again with medication, but I just didn't take enough. I fell asleep until late on a Sunday afternoon when my pastor called to find out why I was not in church that morning. He telephoned my girls, but they did not know how to help me.

There was one time the kids were coming to the house to help me clean up the yard.   I was curled in the corner of the couch when they arrived. My normal curled up, under the covers, comfortable position. I was not in the mood or wanting to get up. My son-in-law Justin literally picked me up and forced me to stand up. He said "You are not to sit on this couch all day while we are here. You will get up and help." I knew he was serious, so reluctantly I forced myself outside to watch them. As soon as they left I was back on the couch in my normal curled up, under the covers, comfortable position.

No one could fix me. I could not understand why Stephanie and Sara could not fix it. Talk to their Dad about going to counseling. At least try. There was no one to turn to. I had no job, my longtime friends were all gone and I had no one to turn to, or lean on except my girls. I finally made the decision to see a Christian counselor, the pastor who married Sara and Justin, another pastor friend, even tried a new church. The Christian counselor and pastor only wanted to work with both of us and that was not going to happen. He had already walked out on the marriage and counseling was not for him. I had been told that so many times before so why ask for this. I wanted it in the worst way because I was not ready to give up on 35 years of marriage. Our marriage was not the best, but we had good times when they were good. I always said to myself when the bad times out did the good then it is time to get out. Not once did I feel we were there. But I guess he felt differently.

When my body finally gave out emotionally, it was recommended that I see a Christian psychiatrist who could help regulate the medications my doctor had given me and to help wean me off of them because I did not like the way they made me feel. I wanted them out of the house. The psychiatrist was able to regulate out my medications after a year so I was at least able to function every day. He was able to slow down the tears. He worked with me and my needs. He was someone who listened and cared enough to help me start the long healing process. Not disguise it, not bury it, but to look at it head on and learn to live with the pain until it became less and less. Does time heal all wounds? To a point it does, but it does not go away fully. It is always there and you just learn to leave it in your past.

During this same time the stress was taking its toll on my heart. My doctor referred me to a heart specialist. My blood pressure was over the limit from the stress and depression. The medication that they added to all the rest, for my heart, was not doing the job fast enough.

The cardiologist wanted me to wear a heart monitor when he found out my heart was coming to complete stops. They would not let me take the regular walking treadmill fearing it would cause more damage so they had me do the one you lie down and they do all the speeding up and slowing down of your heart. I did not pass that test so they scheduled a heart catheterization which showed an area of my heart was not working – calling it "Sick Sinus Syndrome" caused by stress. Now it is known as Broken Heart Syndrome or Stress Cardiomyopathy. I was literally dying of a broken heart. I was told I may need a pacemaker but this was delayed due to the doctor making sure nothing else was happening and he could rule out that I was not just having panic attacks. By the end of the year my health deteriorated even worse and on December 21, 2004 (three months after the judge declared our divorce final) I was scheduled for the pacemaker. When I walked into the hospital that day my heart rate was 28 and my oxygen was 30. Whoa – I was dying. The doctor didn't even know how I walked into the hospital that day.

While dealing with my heart I had one appointment after another with the attorney regarding the settlement of the divorce. It was not going well. No alimony. Nothing. Just a lump sum settlement is all he wanted to do and it would be over. On September 21, 2004 we were to meet with the magistrate to see if everything was in order. Sitting in the hallway of the courthouse with my attorney they came and told us she was not available and that if we waited the judge would see us. It would be over, settled just like that. I was not prepared mentally for it to end on this day. I was so angry I started to nitpick items left in the Lake Erie property that I wanted trying to delay the hearing. If Pat would not agree then I would walk out. When we finally got into the judge's chambers listening to the questions he was asking and the answers that Pat was giving, all I could do was lay my head on the table and cry. Over…done…just like that 34 years down the drain.

I continued to ask myself again what was happening. What was going on? Why? Where do I turn to now that the rope I was hanging onto was gone. Satan had pulled me into his clutches so tight I could not breathe. I couldn't even let God fully in to bring me some peace. That's all I cried out for now. Feeling sorry for myself until one day I FULLY committed to God to set me free of this pain, to give me strength and purpose to move forward and live my life to the fullest.

I cried out as loud as I could to God. Only this time on my knees, openly and not behind closed doors. I was weeping for answers not knowing how or why God should help me now…..a closet Christian who had failed Him in so many ways. I was someone who had walked away from Him again and again. But God did hear my prayers.

First He had removed the issue of the lump in my breast knowing that this was more than I could bear at this time. GOD can heal!

After praying and praying and listening for two years God was working full time in my life and my prayers were being answered. My strength was returning, the tears had nearly come to an end and I was able to function day to day. The pacemaker worked immediately. I don't think I would have made it another 30 days. I praise God everyday for giving me the will to live again.

"Guard your heart more than any

treasure, for it is the source of

all life."

Proverbs 4:23 NEB

Chapter 5

Single

Scared

And Alone with God

I dedicate this chapter to Pat who

gave me the freedom

To again walk with God.

When I fell to my knees, I asked God for help by turning to Him and fully submitting myself to Him, as I was--broken. He started giving me passages from the Bible to get me through the hard and difficult days to help me find comfort in his word.

Cast your cares on the LORD
and he will sustain you;
he will never let
the righteous be shaken.

Psalms 55:22 NIV

God was the only one I could trust because it seemed everyone else had walked away. I was single at 54 with a mid life crisis in full tilt. Rejected and discarded by the one you loved and lived with for 34 years, raised your children with, simply gone and only saying, "I no longer love you".

As always, I was asking myself 'why' did I do the things I did and 'why' I could not stay honest in the marriage. Question after question, with no answers in sight, I am convinced I am not to find those answers because God will answer them for me someday. But I continued to beat myself up day after day.

Single and alone, confused, scared, panic-stricken, and petrified at what life ahead would bring because the world I formally lived in was gone. That which I had made myself comfortable in had come to an abrupt end with just a rap of a gavel, over just like that. How can it be so simple to walk in a courtroom and a marriage of over 34 years be over in an instant?

I had been dependant on Pat for most of my adult life so now what was I going to do now? So alone – Stephanie and Sara had lives and families of their own, and lived over an hour's drive away. They both had been out of the house for almost 10 years. So "empty nest" had set in again, only this time there was no one to share it with. Oh, the pain was so excruciating that the tears flowed continuously. I was still spinning out of control, spinning so fast I was beyond dizzy. I lost complete control of my life.

Scared of the unknown world out there, my safety net was gone. The people that befriended me kept telling me to "let it go", move on, and that Pat wasn't worth my time. They just did not want to understand MY pain. How scared I was with the feelings of rejection and betrayal from Pat, but also from all my long time friends, his family and especially my best friend. Many have called it the "double whammy". I cannot adequately describe how it felt to me except numbness.

Only God knew the full extent of my pain and what I was feeling and He began to show me how to cope with it. God rescued me by finding a family pastor friend who talked to me endless hours any time of the day and night, many times sitting in my basement to talk, so Pat could not overhear our conversations. God also brought four new Christian friends into my life that also prayed endless hours with me and showed how God's love would help heal me if I would just ask. They didn't give up on me as God doesn't give up on us.

They knew what I needed and were showing me how to fill the void through the love of Christ. They told me about a weekend of spiritual renewal call the Emmaus Walk and on July 24th 2004 God held me in His arms and I renewed my relationship with him, openly and faithfully. The walk was very emotional, but I got what I needed to get from it. GOD! Also, some awesome new friends came into my life.

God also brought a young man named Hank into my life that became like a son I never had, and he lived with me for six months. He was my rock and he would hold me hours on end to try and comfort me. He never had to say anything, but with him just being there in the house was like having a guardian angel sent to me by God. I still look at him that way today.

He continues to call and check-in to see how I am doing. I comforted him when he lost his mother. This was just 2 days before my pacemaker surgery. How I drove the 10-hour round trip that Saturday God can only answer. Between Springfield and Dayton I was calling people to come and get me along the highway, but no one was home. I told God He would have to gave me the strength to get myself home. Remember my oxygen was below 50 and my heart rate was dropping rapidly.

Flying Solo is a slow and painful healing. Just to find purpose again in my life. The long journey out of that dark tunnel had begun. God had saved me from committing suicide twice, helped me through rejection of family and longtime friends, MAJOR depression, and my health and heart issues.

God continued to give me new strength to push through my pain and to cope with all the roller coaster emotions that I was feeling. The first thing He showed me was PATIENCE. This was all I could hear from him. All I wanted was to know when would it all end and when would the healing begin?

"But these things I plan won't happen right away. Slowly, Steadily,

surely, the time approaches when the vision will be filled.

If it seems slow, do not despair, for these things will surely come to pass.

Just be Patient!

They will not be overdue a single day."

Habakkuk 2:3

The Living Bible "The Way"

This bible verse became a daily read because patience was not easy. I needed answers, I wanted them now but I soon learned and it sunk in that it is in His time not mine. It had, I just couldn't see or feel it. When I think back over the last 2 years and all the events that happened with the separation and divorce, losing long time friends, my job and my health, I realize today God was taking my life into His hands, and in a new direction. The life I had prayed for in that closet was gone and was not going to be with the people I thought were to be part of those prayers so long ago.

"For I know the plans I have for you
declares the Lord,

plans to prosper you and not harm you,

plans to give you hope and a future.

Then you will call upon me
and come and pray,

to me, and I will listen to you.

You will seek me and find me when you seek

ME with all your heart."

Jeremiah 29: 11-13 NIV

God is leading me in a new direction far better, far greater than I could have ever imagined with patience, forgiveness and unconditional love. Taking one step at a time and learning to put all my trust in Him. God freed me of my own self destruction and is helping me bring down the walls I am building around my heart so determined not to let anyone else in. That pain is too great to go through again. But God opened my mind and ears to listen and accept His unconditional love and not dwell on the ones that had hurt me.

In my alone time I have learned to love myself again and the person that I have become. Walking through that tunnel of darkness and finally being able to see the light at the end called HOPE. To love myself as God loves me.

"God, You've kept track of every toss and turn through sleepless nights, each tear entered in Your ledger, each ache written in Your book."

Psalm 55:22 The Message

46

I found the truth by surviving with God at my side. It is the only way to moving ahead. Learning to enjoy what's ahead for me and not looking back the same way that I did. I've let go of my depression, the hopelessness, anger, and am facing all my emotions, but not without God's guidance. I deserve the best God can give me and I'm reaching out for it.

"In all your ways know, recognize,

acknowledge him, and he will

direct and make straight and plan

your path."

Proverbs 3:6 Amplified

Chapter 6

From above the Clouds

     Dedicated to God for showing me

                the strength to

Start a new life.......

    The time had come for me to try and start a new life. I sold my home, I had lived in for 27 years, and left the town that we had lived in since we were married. I moved to Cincinnati, Ohio; because I had support with Sara and Justin and his family lived there. I was going to the big city to start over. No friends, no job, and no church—living off the money from the sale of my home. All my personal belongings were jammed into a 2-bedroom apartment. I brought my chocolate lab Shelby with me, yet I felt alone again. It felt like I was dumped on the door step to figure everything out. Screaming, what did I do? I left my new friends in Greenville that had stuck by me, my new church, and a new job.

I knew that it was imperative to find a church for me to continue my faith walk with God, or I probably would have walked away again. Jesus held my hand when I walked into Cornerstone Methodist. Quietly I sat and listened not sure if this was what I wanted. I sure was not ready to this was what I wanted. I sure was not ready to step out and greet anybody new? But I did and introduced myself to the singles team. That worked for a while but I was not getting what I needed. I started attending a Sunday school class, and was also invited to a Wednesday Evening Bible group of single women.

I soon started helping in the Divorce Care Ministry with Movin' On ministry that helps singles find strength to move ahead after divorce. It supports them in their healing, and to make sense of their new lives.

Before I moved to Cincinnati, I heard about "Life Coaching" and I investigated it before I left Greenville, but the information was put away when packing. God continued to give me ideas of what I should be doing. He wanted me to help others struggling from divorce or other issues in their lives. I remembered about the information I had on "Life Coaching" so I looked for those papers and returned to the web site of Life Purpose Institute. I called them and asked a lot of questions on what life coaching was about and it seemed to be a fit on trying to help others. I waited until the last minute to register but God opened the door for me to go. There was a cancellation and I ventured out of my box and flew across country to San Diego, California (actually I was beachfront in LaJolla) against everyone's better judgment. I had to keep telling myself it was time for me and I needed to get away to see and do something different. I told everyone it wasn't about them. This was my new adventure. I was looking for my life purpose. I needed time away to look at what was ahead and prove to myself I was somebody. There I was single and a woman scared to death, but off in the wild blue yonder to seek my life's purpose. I was trying to begin the healing process. I knew I had made some strides, but not enough. It was such a slow process and God was teaching me patience. I was willing to try anything to heal the pain.

Here are some of my journal pages:

My flight has begun and I am having a conversation with God while looking out the window. Asking for safe travel and to show me the wisdom, courage and to give me strength to stay out of the box.

The sky is full of clouds, I am not able to see the ground below. Did you know that flying above the clouds gives you a different perspective on life? Watching the clouds from above while talking to God, I was using the peaks and valleys, the smooth and the ripples as parts of my life. Oh, how we all have them, some more than others. I was trying to let go of some, put others in perspective and save some of the good ones. (My marriage was not completely bad. There were good times, too. But when you're faced with starting a new life you must look at it all and I was looking anxiously to the future.)

Asking myself those questions again--What did I do wrong? What could I have done differently? What did I do right? Why? Why her? Why did he pick that time to do it? Trying to figure out the answers I wanted to hear, not always what I <u>needed</u> to hear. Praying and talking to God to find out what the next the next chapter in my life was going to be.

I reached for a magazine in my bag and pulled out an issue of "Enjoying Everyday Life" from the Joyce Meyers Ministries dated May 2005. The very first article by Joyce was 'Develop the Powerful Potential in You". The first sentence read, "Potential is greatness that exists as a possibility but is not yet a reality." Wow – I am heading to a new potential in my life and it is not a reality yet. Isn't that what I'm doing-- finding out my potential in a new career? In the article was a bible verse that had become one of my favorites:

"But those who wait upon God get fresh strength.

They spread their wings and soar like eagles,

They run and don't get tired,

They walk and don't lag behind."

Isaiah 40:31 The Message

God is hitting me between the eyes. I've learned about patience, now he wants me to spread my wings and soar like an eagle. So I'm on my way. I'm asking God for divine guidance to find the peace and joy and purpose He has for me.

Just like her last paragraph in the article states "Whatever your gifts and calling, entrust it to the Lord, pray for his blessing, and develop it. Remember, your times are in His hands and He makes a decision right now that you are not going to be satisfied with anything less than all you can be."

I finished the entire magazine while talking to God when I got to the last article titled, "Starting Early" by Dr. John Maxwell. Although his article says to "start early" I thought about myself. He said " you should be settled in life and career by forty." Here it goes – I'm starting too LATE – I'm making life changing 'major' decisions at 56 leading me to believe I was doing the right thing. My life decisions have not been my choice and as the saying goes, "We have to work with what's dealt to us" and that's what I'm doing with God's help.

But as I was finishing his article he brought up the question I was thinking "What if you've already passed even the forty-five milestone?" Now that I am well past that too….Well, he answered it for me. It's not too LATE to start over! One of his favorite quotes is "Though you cannot go back and make a brand new start, my friend, anybody can start from now and make a brand new end!" Wow, I was pursuing something that would enhance my later years of life. Doing God's work.

I'm searching for my purpose and potential in my life and NOW IS THE TIME!

The sun has set on the Pacific and I'm such at peace with myself. I'm hoping for a good night's sleep because tomorrow is going to be a day of adventure.

Good morning. It is Tuesday and I am watching while the streets and park below come alive with people. Swimmers are in the water, walkers are strolling along the beach and kayakers are paddling away watching and listening to God's world. I am getting ready to walk for the day and enjoy my time. I found a small Catholic Mission Church that was 100 years old with its doors wide open inviting me in. I quietly went in to pray and admire the beautiful structure. If walls could talk I am sure they could tell some wonderful stories. God is so good to me.

I began the Life Coaching classes and was able to find more peace and purpose for my life. While there I would be celebrating Sara's birthday away from her. My daughter who I almost didn't get to raise after her birth. Her birthday is always difficult for me, because I remember the trauma of her birth. But this birthday was different. Two new friends, Stephanie and Mark, stayed with me all day and took me out for supper surprising me with a cake at the Hard Rock Café. They wanted to celebrate the life that God gave me. Not the trauma of coming close to losing my life. You know, no one had ever told me to celebrate my still being here. That's what coaching is all about, and they practiced on me.

God wants me to help others in their time of need. Just like Stephanie and Mark did for me. Make a positive out of a negative. Be there to listen with compassion, empathy, and respect. The week came to a close too fast, but it was time to pack up with a new sense of knowledge of what I was to do.

On my flight home the answer was clear, not a cloud in the sky. It was so beautiful below that I could see God's patchwork quilt. I wrote how the clouds were peaks and valleys of my life and I was going to California to find my "Life's purpose". I did--I found reason, I found life purpose, I found some of the answers I had been looking for, I found new friends and a support group that is the greatest.

Now I just want my daughters to understand and get to know who I am….

Chapter 7

Mom

Dedicated to my daughters Stephanie and Sara

Now the task at hand is what do we do with MOM? I know that question was very real to both the girls. Mom is alone. She is devastated and we do not know how to help her. I can tell you they tried to be there for me, but not at the times I felt I needed them the most. We didn't live in the same towns and they could not be with me or see me day by day, to truly see how I was doing. They tried to comfort me the best they knew how by phone, but I knew they were suffering, too. The family they knew was gone. They were put in the middle those first months, and now I so regret that.

How do you describe the pain that was cut so deep that I could not breathe, could not move, or the feeling of being a failure to them? Trying to explain to them what I was going through? He had moved on and was getting along just fine. Talking things out was never an option for me in the past, and now when I could talk without fearing any repercussions I just could not tell them all that I felt. I could only give those bits and pieces of what I truly wanted them to know. I still feel that way today as I find it very difficult to talk to them about what is going on in my life because they feel it is always about me.

One of the hardest things was I couldn't ask them how they were doing like a Mom should. They had to also deal with their father leaving their mother for someone that had been part of their lives for years too. They were being told my friend tried to close the door, but Pat kept coming back. I could not reach out and comfort them. I cried to them a lot, but they could not answer me or if they did I could not hear and I knew they could not give me back my family. The one thing I wanted. The life my best friend split apart along with their Dad. So what's next?

What I heard were comments like, "This is for the best", "Move on it's over", "He's moved on, why can't you?", "You need to find someone else", "Mom we want you to find someone who will respect you for who you are", on and on. I wanted their comfort, not words of letting go. I wanted them to just hold me and let me cry in their arms. I wanted to be held just once. I needed them to say they had forgiven me for the lies and deceit that occurred. How could I explain to them all I was feeling?

I'll admit that we did not have the perfect marriage,

but we were a family for 34 years. Maybe dysfunctional, but so many families are and you learn to make the best of it. You're happy when you're happy and you're miserable when you're miserable, but you make it work when you need to. So many families live this way even though it is not God's way. It is called survival and that is exactly how I lived. I valued my vows "for better or for worse" and "till death do us part". We were married in God's eyes and even though I had become a closet Christian I believed in those two things.

But I was still asking myself questions. Those good old "why" questions "Why do I feel so worthless?" "Why was I such a failure?" "Why does everything I do go wrong?" "Why can't I be happy?" "Why can't my family be whole again?" Why, Why, Why, why, why…… We have all been there sometime in our lives, but now I needed answers. I had become a victim engulfed in my own pain, denial, and agony. I was looking for answers that no one could seem to give me. Pat was not talking to me, my girlfriend (I thought was my girlfriend) hung up on me, his family walked away, and my side of the family did what they could.

But I was also asking myself what is best for my girls and their families? They wanted me to move out of my home that I had lived in for over 25 years because of the memories and coming there for them was just too hard. But I was confused how they could still go to our vacation home at Lake Erie with their Dad and his girlfriend and how the memories there would be any different.

I felt like I had to make all the changes to satisfy my girls. I lost holidays as a family. I gave up the home I felt safe in. I lost the lifestyle I grew accustomed to. There was no fight left in me to argue. If I had it to do over, some of my choices would have been different. They could accept his new lifestyle, but not how I was living. Where would I fit in by myself?

We were a family "together" and now became the split life of two separate family functions. Question after question, I was still asking myself. But the hardest of this all is the choices that my girls had to make. My heart cries for them every time they plan a birthday party for the grandkids, the birth of new grandkids, christenings, holidays, etc. They want us to be able to be in the same room together, but that will probably never happen. (Today I can say it is not my choice. I would be fine with it, but they seem to make that choice that we will not be at the same function together anymore.)

Re-inventing my life was now at hand. The task of what do I do now. How do I become a new person, an independent person, an individual who has to make my own decisions regarding what is best for me ?

How do I become a better Mom?

To be a person that God and I both like, as well as those around me and one my daughters can be proud of. God found a way for me to take baby steps and now I am taking wider strides for him. I attend church regularly, taken and taught divorce recovery, other healing classes to find strength for myself and others. I am doing what I am supposed to do to heal correctly. "Why" do I still feel so bad at times and "Why" did I create this wall so far and so high around my heart determined not to let anyone else in?

The pain and emptiness is too great to go through again. But God has entered and I am listening to how He will protect me. Reality hurts, but reality will set you free. He is making me whole through my faith, and I am praising His glory to continue to give me strength to grow and live the rest of my life happy, with or without someone.

"Consider it wholly joyful, my brethren,
whenever you are enveloped in or encounter
trials of any sort or fall into various
temptations.

Be assured and understand that the
trial and proving of your faith bring
out endurance and steadfastness and patience.
James 1:2-3 Amplified

But how do I re-invent myself in my mid fifties and continuing into my sixties to make myself attractive to others? God has given me a chance to redesign my life. A new life, a new me, and new independence is what God has given me, a chance to find out who I am as a person, a friend, and especially a MOM. I may have failed to be God's child before, but he has given me a chance to start over with His approval. I am taking time for self-reflection and self-improvement. Finding out who I am and the person I should be. I buried myself over 35 years ago, when I needed self-acceptance. But first I had to get right with God. It has taken 40 years. He is changing my life for the better, and desires me to become the best I possibly can. As far as being MOM, my girls have their own families now and they don't seem to need MOM anymore. I desire their forgiveness and receive their love when they can give it to me.   I could not handle it if they walked out of my life too, but there are days when it feels like it. Even though Stephanie and Sara have not had the full effect of this new me—one day I pray they will understand and acknowledge what I have become with all the hopes and dreams that are ahead of me.

I took care of my family for so many years in their ups and downs to protect them and now I thought I wanted them to take care of me. I keep saying I need things from the girls, but I don't know where to begin to ask them besides having patience and understanding with me until I can be MOM again to them. The pain will last as long as it has to, but as each day passes into months and now year's things are taking on new light.

My move to Cincinnati has been positive as far as opportunities to do things and reaching out to others. I had to reach out and make new friends--ones you can trust, those who you can cry to, pray with, and those who do not judge your feelings or your pain. I believe I'm not good enough for someone else because I was so untrue in my last relationship. I was so unable to live in the real world. God is teaching me how to live openly with others and maybe someday I will let someone else enter my heart and live life on God's terms. Find the right person God wants me to have and to accept love again from someone God has brought forth. The one who will love me unconditionally, not on my terms, or on his, but only on God's? I have to stop analyzing what happened, and start living in faith and LET GOD do His thing in my life.

Although my relationship with Stephanie and Sara seems strained at times. We are all working on it. I need them to say they are proud of me for the growth and progress I have made and that they are here to help me when I need it unconditionally. Sometimes just a phone call would be all it would take. Friends have told me I am expecting too much; they don't have enough time. I have been disappointed many times, but I continue to pray with God's help maybe before it's too late I will hear and feel what I need from them both. It needs to be sincere and not just words to satisfy me.

Chapter 8

Rays of Hope

Dedicated to those who have found their Ray of

Hope and peace to begin their new LIFE....

Coming out of that long tunnel of darkness you finally see those "Rays of Hope". "Time heals all wounds" is an old saying, but I read somewhere it should be, "Time changes all wounds". Finding peace during adversity is difficult. But turning yourself towards God and listening to his commands can GIVE you the peace you need within yourself. Without God in my life, there would have been no hope, no changes, and no healing.

"Then what am I to do? I will pray with my spirit,

but I will also pray with my mind and understanding;

I will sing with my spirit,

but I will sing with my mind and understanding also."

I Corinthians 14:15 Amplified

God and I are pretty tight, and that will never change no matter who comes into my life. I am trying to do what God asks of me on a day to day basis. He is the only One I can trust at this time and the only One I can rely on. I never thought I was going to be that divorced woman, but I'm here and God is turning my pain into something positive for me and the lives I am touching.

God is showing me new ministry opportunities to help others to heal. Through teaching different healing classes. Seeing someone smile for the first time whose heart is breaking gives me such joy. Just knowing that I have touched their heart with kind words, or a smile or even a listening ear may be all it takes. This helps me with my healing, too. I pull from their strength and they pull from mine. I cannot erase their pain because only God can do that, but I sure can ease the pain a little. We all need help during life's crises and we must not be afraid to ask for help. We all need to have a shoulder to cry on – someone who will listen – that one person who you could shed those ever flowing tears too. (I call them cleansing tears) – the one who just let's you let out saying nothing.

So many women are left alone during midlife that I want to give them hope that life can go on for another good 20 plus years. They have to learn they can be happy with themselves and those around them. Show them how to find the strength to get right with themselves and God. I so strongly advise them to find their strength in Him. He is the only One who can heal them!

It is so easy just to run from everything, bury yourself under the covers, and hide your feelings because you believe everyone has turned against you. Many others run from God. That is the wrong direction and thought pattern to heal. Instead, we need to run to God for He is waiting with open arms to hold and comfort us.

"He comes alongside us when we go

through hard times,

and before you know it,

he brings us alongside someone else

who is going through hard times so

that we can be there for that

person just as God was there for us."

2 Corinthians 1:34 The Message

When God catches you He comforts you. He holds you. He guides you. He will help you live your life full of passion with strength and courage. He listens when no one else does. He encourages you in your down times. He catches every tear you shed and saves them. He knows your heart, soul, and mind inside and out. So why not try God? He told me in one of my favorite bible verse it was time for me to!

"But those who wait upon GOD get fresh strength.

They spread their wings and soar like eagles,

They run and don't get tired,

they walk and don't lag behind."

Isaiah 40:31 The Message

I am soaring on my own. I still have to make choices that are difficult, but there is hope that I can continue to make the right choices that are good for me and the family I have left. My future peace depends on it. I can't worry anymore about what happened in the past, and I can't really control my future either. But I can live victoriously with God at my side controlling the present and what is happening today, this hour, this minute, this second. I still have difficult times because you never know what will trigger a difficult moment.

One of those times was just seeing the family

Christmas ornaments on my daughter's Christmas tree that caused me to abruptly leave her home with no explanation. Crying all the way home because those ornaments should have been on my family tree in my family home. But that was all gone now. Something as trivial as that could set me off. In those times God comforts me and tells me it will be okay, and I must be patience. He has to remind me on a day-to-day basis to stay calm, put one foot in front of the other, and my peace and happiness will return. Keep "moving ahead" and heal the healthy way.

With God's unconditional love He is showing me what true happiness can be which leads me to share with others His love and grace. He is giving me the missing pieces and helping me to be happy now by living life to the fullest, whole. I receive his joy everyday with the time I have left here on earth.

God has restored my brokenness, and is healing my heart to give me a new beginning. He is healing my memories with truth and not judging me. He has forgiven me for what I did with the lies and deceit during my marriage.

But what about forgiveness towards Pat and my best friend? That did not come easy. How or why should I? All I wanted to do was get even. The only person I was only really hurting was me. Until one day God spoke to me through something I read, "Make peace with yourself and I will take care of the rest. There will be times when the pain and hurt will come back, maybe with a vengeance but your life is in my hands and you are following my lead everyday – you're only hurting yourself because THEY DON'T CARE – do not waste your time – do my work and receive the glory I have for you". WOW, this was so powerful to me that I kept repeating this over and over in my head "vengeance is mine," saith the Lord and THEY DON'T CARE.

Corrie Ten Boom has a beautiful quote that sums it up pretty good. "Forgiveness is the key which unlocks the door of resentment and the handcuffs of hatred. It breaks the chains of bitterness and the shackles of selfishness."

I would throw my own pity parties that only I could attend and I hate to say I had too many to count. I could not continue to live filled with guilt and despair, or the feelings of anger and bitterness any longer. God commands us to restore ourselves for Him as told in Matthew 18:21-22.

Then Peter came to Him and said,

"Lord, how many times shall I forgive my

brother or sister who sins against me?

Up to seven times?"

Jesus said to him,

"I tell you, not seven times,

but seventy times seven."

Matthew 18: 21-22 NIV

God gave me the strength to forgive so that I could move forward. He told me the days of shouting are over and He will give me rest, I have bigger and better things planned for you! So I laid down the past. He continues to help me get rid of my pain, my feeling of emptiness by being there for me. God's love never fails or quits. I did fail God, but He hasn't failed me. I have to let go of the guilt about the "what ifs" or "should haves" that would have made it better or different. I know Pat didn't want to seek help because I tried. You can't help someone who doesn't want it. I did my best with what I had, right or wrong and it's over. One thing I do know, God will not let me make the same mistakes again as long as He is part of my life. This book is not about Pat, but about my struggles to heal and begin my new life. God gave me grace, amazing, wonderful, redeeming and loving GRACE. My sins are forgiven. So I stopped beating myself up because I deserve God's best. True forgiveness is the most freeing and peaceful feeling you can ever have.

No one in any class I have taken, support group I have attended, or book I have read has told me how to turn off the love I still have for Pat. I continue to forgive him and I pray for him to seek help to heal and to find God in his heart. If someday God leads him back to me through God's help maybe we can begin the long process of starting our lives all over again as friends. This has been my prayer.

"Truly I tell you, if anyone says to this mountain,
'Go, throw yourself into the sea,' and does not
doubt in their heart but believes that what they
say will happen, it will be done for them.
Therefore I tell you, whatever you ask for in
prayer, believe that you have received it,
and it will be yours. And when you stand
praying, if you hold anything against anyone,
forgive them, so that your Father in heaven may
forgive you your sins."
Mark 11:23-26 NIV

This book is just a part of my healing. I HOPE that it may help just one other person find a "ray of hope" to continue living the life God wants for them.

LET THE HEALING BEGIN AT LAST!!!!!!!

Chapter 9

God's Healing Touch Again

2011 began like any other year. I had set some new goals. You know the usual ones--to lose weight, get out of debt, draw closer to God, and de-clutter my condo. I still have boxes unopened from my move to Cincinnati. I needed to go through them. Just like the others, these resolutions were short-lived. By the end of January I wasn't feeling well and had a painful rash starting on my left side. Finally the pain was so severe I needed to find out what was going on. Because I had no doctor I went to Urgent Care and the doctor confirmed I had shingles. It took nearly a month to get over them. They were terrible and painful and I hope I never get them again.

The year seemed to be going along well after that. I had been in my condo for a year. Then on July 28th my hiatal hernia decided to rear its ugly head. I had not had many issues with it since the divorce. I was out with a friend and we were discussing an email I had received earlier that day that had upset me when I started choking. I would never know when it would decide flare up. I went to the bathroom like I would always do and it did not stop.

This time it was different and it would not settle down. After getting home Ron wanted to take me to the ER, but I told him I would be okay. It would eventually stop. Instead I was up all night. I tried walking outside at 6 a.m. I was still not able to swallow and if I drank something it would just come right back up. I went to Urgent Care again because I still did not have a family doctor. I asked for medicine to settle it down because I was leaving town to go to Pennsylvania that afternoon and needed for this to stop. It did not work.

By 1 p.m. I was still dry-heaving and I knew I was in trouble. I drove myself to the ER and called my friend Janie to meet me. I also called the girls who were planning on going to Pennsylvania. I didn't want to call my daughters because I felt it was something simple that needed to be done, and I would be out the door and on my way to Pennsylvania.

They did x-rays and had difficulty getting an IV in my veins because I was dehydrated. Finding nothing they decided to call a gastroenterologist doctor. They said he would be finishing up another surgery soon and thereafter would be taking me in to be scoped. I told Janie I thought it was time to call Sara and my church.

Everything went fast and they found that a piece of steak had lodged itself in my esophagus. After removing it, the doctor wanted to schedule more testing on the hiatal hernia and stretch my throat in two weeks. He informed me this would be needed three times because I was so restricted and he would not be able to do it at one time.

The upper GI exam was completed and when I met with the doctor the news was not good. My stomach had moved completely through my diaphragm and was ripped in half. It turned upside down causing my hiatal hernia to become a very dangerous par esophageal hernia. I was in serious trouble.

When I went in for the second throat stretching, on the bed ready to start, my blood pressure went through the roof. The doctor canceled the procedure and said I needed to see an MD immediately. I didn't have one, but while on the bed he called a friend of his that got me in right away. It was the day before Labor Day and the new MD was leaving town, but he would stay to see me. If I had not been able to see him they would have kept me in the hospital. My blood pressure was over the 200/180 mark and they cannot explain why I did not have a stroke. I was immediately put on medication and bed rest for the week end.

I returned to the gastroenterologist to be referred to another surgeon for the repair of my par esophageal hernia. I saw the new doctor in mid-September, but he would not schedule the surgery until my blood pressure was down. It was a long 6 weeks until he was finally able to schedule my surgery for November 8th. I was afraid to eat and I was on a soft diet. This lady's meat days are over.

Even though I was scared to death, I had a peace inside because my faith in God and that He would take care of me. I had several surgeries in my lifetime, but when he explained just how serious this one is and what the procedure was to fix it I was scared. He did not know if he would have to completely open up my chest or be able to do it laparoscopically. He was hoping he could perform the surgery laparoscopically because it would be so much easier on me, but it would all depend on how much damage there was.

The day came and my daughters accompanied me to the hospital along with my friends Janie, church friend Karen and Bob. I wanted Janie there to be with my girls just in case things got bad. We discussed my wishes in the car and I gave them all my directives with a signed medical power of attorney and living will.

Surgery started and actually went well and the doctor was able to perform it laparoscopically, but I was in trouble from the CO_2 they had used when it exploded in my chest. There was a pocket left when they moved my lung back into position to try and inflate it. The doctor was at my side from 8:30 a.m. until 8 p.m. not knowing if I was going to make it. This was only the second time something like this had happened to him. I am thankful he stayed with me, because I don't think I would have made it.

The next thing I remember is they were trying to get a chest tube in my side and I realized something was inserted down my throat. I started biting on it and the nurse explained it was a ventilator to help me breathe. I was in serious trouble. What happened? What was going on? I could not open my eyes and I tried to talk. They were talking about bringing Stephanie and Sara in, but they would have to explain what they were going to see. I heard them talk about how swollen I was and that explained why I could not open my eyes. When I was later able to talk to the doctor he told me there was no way I could remember him putting the chest tube in because he had all the sedative in me he could give me or it would have killed me. I did not feel any pain, but felt his hand open up my side and go through my rib cage to insert the tube.

When they brought the girls in I was able to see through tiny slits. There stood Stephanie at the foot of the bed. I knew it was her, but I could not make out her expression and I am sure it scared both of them. I knew what they were seeing because I remember seeing my former father-in-law swollen after a surgery. Stephanie later told me my eyes were the size of golf balls.

They drove my mother down to see me on Wednesday night and I am glad that by then they had taken out the ventilator. I would not have wanted her to see me that way. I do remember her coming with my sister Jana and her husband Bill, but that is all. I was told I had other visitors but I don't remember any of them along with Pastors from the church. I guess I was not a pretty sight. An overnight stay turned into 5 days on oxygen because they were trying to get air back into my lung slowly. Also, my sugar went out of control and they were giving me insulin. I was a mess, and really didn't care. When I was finally able to go home on Saturday I went to Sara's for the rest of the weekend and Stephanie would come down on Monday and stay with me for a couple of days.

When I met with the doctor after surgery, I was told my lifestyle of eating and singing in church choir was going to change. He informed me I had to eat small meals throughout the day and I was not allowed to sing anymore. But I told him that was in God's hands not mine or his. I was still afraid to eat too much anyway so this I could manage. Leaving the choir was a different story and very hard for me. He said if I ever ripped my diaphragm again it would not be an easy fix. I did not like how my life would change. I have lost over 60 pounds and I eat about half of what I used to do. I have not returned to choir and I miss it so much, but I sing with them in spirit every Sunday.

Losing the weight has been a good thing and on the whole I feel really great. There are times I have issues with my pacemaker or my stomach and eating, but I am making the best of it and I am thankful I'm still here to enjoy what life I have left.

I have had several talks with God since, that it was time to reveal His plan to me now because I am not going through this kind of scare again. This one was too close and I know He saved me again just as He did when I had Sara, and a previous surgery before I had my girls. People tell me I must have nine lives and I have spent 3 of them and I tell them I am done....no more. It's is time to get on with my life and live it.

Chapter 10

Peace After a Shattered Life

Dedicated to those who have found PEACE

with themselves to start a new life.

Finding peace during adversity is difficult – but turning yourself towards God and listening to his commands can give you the peace you need within yourself.

That's difficult when all you want to do is run from everything. When everyone has turned against you, so you think, you want to turn away from God. In the middle of your pain God will give you purpose.

"And after you have suffered a little while, the God of all grace, who has called you to His eternal glory in Christ, will himself restore, confirm, strengthen, and establish you."

1 Peter 5:10 ESV

You have the God given right to be happy again. I have made something very devastating and negative into something very positive by helping others. Sharing my story of survival and learning not to give up because so many just want to give up like I wanted to do or jump into new relationships too soon. Healing your heart is important and needs to be done correctly. Taking the time is well worth it and renewing your faith in God is a sure thing.

It has been 11 years since my divorce, and I feel the hardest part of the journey is behind me. When I was told in Divorce Care that it takes 1 year for every 4 years you are married I could not believe that it would take me 9 years to heal. But I will tell you it has taken every bit of it and more! It has not been an easy road. I must be honest I do still have my days. Those long weekends when I have no plans or during the holidays. But I push through and get mad at myself for throwing a pity party. Loneliness is not easy and is painful. I am not going to say this will ever end because I am still having them. I just hope with each passing year it gets easier.

I want to share some of my journal pages throughout this journey. I wish I had done more journaling and I would highly recommend it. But it was just too painful at times.

Journal Entry – August 13, 2004

Words cannot explain how I feel. I made Pat remove more of his stuff today. I have to get it out of the house so I can continue to move forward. This is so hard.

I have to continue my walk and work for the Lord to help others. My comfort and strength comes from you Lord, and I am so thankful I found you again. Each day seem to get easier and when this is over I truly know it is for the best. Then there are other days that the tears just don't stop. Help me Lord and give me strength.

Journal Entry - February 19, 2005

It's been awhile. Last evening I was given a challenge that might help put my life in order. It has 4 categories (1) Personal Health (2) Key Relationships (3) Job (4) Life Mission. I want to give it a try because nothing seems to be working right now. Please Lord; continue to give me strength to go on!

(This did give me some points to think about and I kept them in front of me for awhile. I was always looking for something that would help the healing process.)

Journal Entry – May 5, 2005

It's been awhile since I wrote and I need to get back to it. Yesterday Stephanie made a comment to me that really bothered me. She said I was a "strong person." I am having doubts about myself again. I have to take my mother to her sister's funeral Friday and I don't have the strength or anyone to lean on. But I do – You Lord are my strength every day. I do know that, but there are times I let you down. I want to be strong all the time, but Satan wants to bring me down. I also know I am a better person than I was a year ago.

Today I was watching Joyce Meyers and what she said hit me. I know I needed to hear it. Satan was attacking me by making me a prisoner in my home again. I am "Complete in Christ." So today I am getting my strength back and telling myself I am okay. As Joyce said "Okay and on my way."

Lord you are my strength and you are in my life every day. You are leading me in the right direction – your purpose is being revealed to me daily even though the doubts come in sometime – You keep me on track – You keep me focused. You love me. I pray this to you. Amen.

Journey Entry – April 6, 2006

Questions to ponder on my move to Cincinnati....

1. Is now the time to make this decision?
    My house is sold and that is what has   kept me from
    making the move to Cincinnati. I pray the doors will
    open for a job and apartment or condo to start this
    journey, a new beginning. I put it all in your hands for
    a new life.

2. What is the purpose of this decision?
    Start a new life – Find out who Linda is

    Be with Sara and family

    Can't seem to move on in Greenville

    Running away

    Peace

    Overcome my fear

    Overcoming my feelings of being a failure

3. What information do I need to make the decision?
    I have all the information I need

4. What are my alternatives? Which is easiest?   Which is
    best?

Alternatives: Can always move back

Easiest: Stay in Greenville and battle

with myself

Best: Move to Cincinnati

Find a job I am happy with

Challenge

Start a new life

You will find that decisions do have to be made and when you are alone they can be very frightening and difficult to make. The Bible says "Don't be afraid!" There are three-hundred sixty-five verses in the Bible that address fear, anxieties, and worries. That is one for each day of the year. So, I know God will make a way.

Journal Entry – December 2, 2006

Well, I'm here and listening to you to begin my notes.

You've been working overtime with me and it is time to put pen in hand with your help. I'm so questioning why you feel I have such a strong story to tell. But I am not to question, but to obey your word.

You have been so clear this past week so here it goes. (It was time to start this book)

Journal Entry - December 31, 2006

This year is finally over and a new year begins tomorrow with another fresh start. Choices have been big for me this year and not all have been right. Tomorrow is another new year and a new day to begin making <u>GOOD CHOICES.</u> With you God leading the way, I will. Just like the message in church this past Sunday. We should ask ourselves "God, what do <u>you</u> want <u>me</u> to do with my life this year?"

I have also found a new quote that is going up on my mirror. "Hope smiles on the THRESHOLD of the year to come, whispering that it will be happier." ~Alfred Lord Tennyson

I'm making goals for 2007, and with your help I can achieve them.

1. Closer walk with God including reading the one year Bible and daily devotional

2. Job
3. Find a new home
4. Lose 20-30 lbs with exercise 3 times per week
5. Work on Coaching
6. Finish writing books – Publish (here it is 2014!)

Journal Entry – February 10, 2007

Here it is February and I have to make a decision on renewing my lease. I still have not found a job and my finances are running out. I am so confused again on staying in Cincinnati. Things are just not what I thought they would be like. Friends are hard to make, a job is hard to find, and I'm miserable again. Of course the 7" of snow hasn't helped either. I keep asking and putting it in God's hands and He just keeps telling me to work on the book. I am so done with it.

Life is so complicated and being alone is so hard. This is my anniversary month and we would have been married 38 years. So much time lost. I would take it back just to have a life…but I know God doesn't want that. God please keep me strong. AMEN!

Journal Entry - February 20, 2007

God you took me literal today when I slammed my fist on my computer desk and said I needed a job today. You knew this was the job for me. <u>You do answer prayers</u>. You knew I was starting to doubt my faith and my abilities, but as always, you know best and I need to practice patience.

This day evolved so fast, but it is so great to finally be at peace with a job. Hopefully this is the job for me. (I have been here for 7 ½ years)

Our God is such an awesome God and you heard my cry. Please continue your work in me. Thank you God for being part of my life every day. AMEN!

Journal Entry – September 10, 2007

I am humbly asking for your help, Lord. I am at the lowest of lows, but still watching you work in my life. I now know the name of the women's ministry you want me to start "Tapestry" (later changed to Patchwork Ministry) to put the pieces back together to make a beautiful quilt.

The game plan has begun so now actions must start. Even though I am low, I feel excitement building as I write this so I know this is it. My pieces are: faith, trust, patience, pain, betrayal, hope, tears, dream, change, forgiveness, priorities, prayer, journey, birth, renewed, joy, blessings, believing, and obedient.

Journal Entry – September 5, 2010

Dear God, Sorry for not journaling like I keep saying I want to do. Today is a new day and I need to write down some thoughts, praises and struggles.

Praises – I am now settled into a new condo – my home – something I can call my own. Thank you Sara and Justin for making this a reality. This has taken so much pressure off me and I can now enjoy my life. Begin living in your honor. I'm here Lord to do your work – I'm yours to do what you need.

For the past few years I didn't feel I could find the peace I have today. Now, this moment. Thank you Lord for giving me patience to grow into the person I am and for your patience with me to move slowly and take the time to grow and heal with myself, my faith and my life. Whatever happens, I owe it all to you.

Struggling – I need your help, Lord. I have prayed about it and now I need help. I feel you have put someone in my life for a reason, and I am struggling with my emotions. The cement wall I have put around my heart is crumbling, and I don't know how to fully understand my feelings.

My fear of rejection. I can't express myself to him for fear he will walk out of my life. Now that I have the opportunity to be open in a relationship I still have fear. I pray you can help me overcome this – please help me open up to him to find out if we will ever move into a more couple type relationship. Please help me Lord!

Thoughts – Life is good and with God in my life it will only get better…..If he is only in my life for a short time I am going to enjoy the time we spend together. God brought him into my life for a reason and a season. (He walked out in 2012, but we are still friends)

Journal Entry - January 1, 2011

Moving forward this year to another level…my resolutions are as follows:

1. More Daily devotional time
2. Journal more
3. Deeper Faith
4. Exercise – walking
5. Lose 30# (little did I know this was going to happen for real.)
6. Better health (little did I know this became a must)
7. Let go of material things
8. Guard my heart
9. Give more of myself to others
10. Love unconditionally
11. Read more, less TV

Please God, please increase my ministry possibilities because I do want to make it a full-time career. Let me see life's situations with new insight by making the right choices...Let me continue to network with others.

I am blessed with my new condo

I am blessed with my girls and their families

I am blessed that I have God in my life

I am blessed for having my mother still here

I am blessed for other family members and a whole lot of friends that I can TRUST

I am blessed for my church and the support they give me.

(I am jumping to 2013 and the start of a "spiritual fast" challenged by our pastor.

Journal Entry – October 15, 2013

Today is the start of my 3 day per week lunch fast. Tues – Wed – Thurs. I will sit quietly for 30 minutes and read my devotional and pray to you God that you continue to show me your plan for my life. God you have been showing me 'bits and pieces' of what you have in store for me and I'm scared, but with you all things are possible. I praise you for being part of my life and blessing me in so many ways.

The cover of this new journal I picked up and the first verse below is a great start to this journey of fasting and prayer in a place that hopefully will respect what I am doing on this "spiritual fast". Thank you Jesus for the blessings you are giving me for my ministry.

Front Cover "I know the plans I have for you," declares the Lord, "plans to prosper you and not to harm you, plans to give you hope and a future." Jeremiah 29:11

Verse at the bottom of the first page "But seek first his kingdom and his righteousness, and all these things will be given to you as well." Matthew 6:33

Last Journey Entry I want to share.

Journal Entry – November 6, 2013

Another WOW day for me today – 10 years since my world turned inside out. You never left me or forsake me and yesterday my strength overwhelmed me regarding how I feel. You have seen my struggles – surrounded me with your love, and the people you have brought in my life have been fantastic. Wow…wow…wow…It is always amazing where you take me on this journey of serving you. You are constantly reminding me of Jeremiah 29:11 "It's your plan" and I love it.

I think I can truly say I'm healed and yes I do have triggers once in awhile that brings it all back but I know God sees me through those time and His abundant love will overflow my cup. I am looking forward to 2014 and the new teachings you are showing me. It's going to be a great year.

My prayers continue for many and only You Lord know their needs…please protect them, give them strength, but most of all hold them in your loving arms like you did for me. I continue to pray for my family as one day they will understand who I am and why I do what I do for you Lord.

Thank you Lord for my everyday blessings, your grace, and your strength! AMEN.

Chapter 11

God's Vision

GOD WILL GIVE YOU THE VISION.

"Call ME and I will answer you

and show you great and mighty things,

fenced in and hidden,

which you do not know"

Jeremiah 33:3

God's vision and plan for my life has come in several different directions. From naming my ministry "Patchwork Ministry", to this book, speaking, facilitating different groups and to being a contributing author to the book "Inspired Women Succeed" as well as my servant hood to others.

The first vision came to me the summer of 2006 in California when God spoke to me about writing 6 books called "simple reads". He gave me six titles to these books.

I failed to act on it, but he came to me again in December when He sat in my car while I was driving to Greenville on a rainy day. He told me to get out pencil and paper and write. I told him I was driving, but he said he has the car in his hands. Finding a scrap piece of paper and writing on the steering wheel while He spoke, He gave me the 6 titles again, along with who they were to be dedicated to, and the first paragraph for each. When I got home that evening I found my notes from the summer and the titles where pretty much the same, but this time he gave me more information to begin writing.

I still did nothing with my notes until January when out loud on a cold and dreary Saturday He commanded me to write not tomorrow or a month from now, but today. I wrote notes for 3 chapters. Still feeling overwhelmed I didn't know what to do, but to investigate how to write a book. He continued to tell me what to write and quit investigate writing. It took me 6 months to get it all together, but not without a lot of prayer and thought as to what I wanted and needed to say.

This book is the writings of those 6 "simple read" books that have become the 11 Chapters of "my story".

Why my story? God

just says "Why not your story? It will touch someone's heart that is breaking and they will find "Hope Among the Tears".

Journal Entry – December 2, 2006

Well, I'm here and listening to you to begin my notes again.

You've been working overtime with me and it is time to put pen in hand with your help. I'm so questioning why you feel I have such a strong story to tell. However, I'm not to question, but obey your words.

You have been so clear this past week, so here it goes. (It has taken until 2015 to finish, but I did it and I know it will help just one person who will read it that through Him all things are possible.)

My second vision happened like this:

God appeared to me again one night when I was sitting in the dark with candles glowing throughout my apartment, because my power had been shut off, and I had an eviction notice in my hand. Praying seemed to be the right thing to do and listen for God's guidance on what to do next. He suddenly appeared in my room and sat beside me on my bed. I was again feeling the lowest of lows with tears streaming down my checks. He was saying "I am with you" but you need to get out pencil and paper again. I knew it was time to listen again. He told me He was naming my healing ministry Patchwork Ministry. He asked me to draw a picture of a quilt I am to make. It is my "healing quilt". I will be using this quilt in my presentations about how to piece our lives back together again.

I drew a picture of the sun with rays of hope and God centered in the middle, as well as all the fears, emotions, and struggles. He continued to direct me by adding a cross and leaving all my burdens at the foot of the cross and the rays of hope spreading from the center of the cross with God centered in the middle. So "Patchwork Ministry" was born. It should be ready to begin the first of the year. He set that as a goal for me and He also said to me "I have given you the tools for you to begin my work so next year you will live in abundance."

Jesus said "I have come so that you

can have life and have it more

abundantly."

John 10:7,10

    I am finally excited about something positive in my life. He is showing me ways to go on with my life and serve him by touching other women to find their "Ray of Hope".

    I look forward to serving God and I thank Him daily for my healing even though I am still His work in progress. God heals those who believe, and sends them out to help others in their time of need. I am blessed to know that this is what I am supposed to do.

"We are assured and know that all things

work together and are for good to

and for those who love God

and are called according to his

design and purpose."

Romans 8:28 AMP

We are called, but we have a choice to listen and obey. God continues to do wonderful things in my life and I receive blessings every day because of it. There are times I still have to ride that emotional roller coaster from life's triggers, but I believe and know God is just showing me I need to completely rely on Him for my peace and my joy.

For me, I am thankful now for all my trials, the roller coaster ride, the mountain I dug through in that dark tunnel with no light....because I can now declare Who Am I!

I am a child of God, wonderfully made, perfectly imperfect, awesomely loved, but most importantly forgiven by God.

AND, OH YES, I LISTEN TO GOD EVERYDAY!!!

Stop and Listen

I stopped and listened
as you spoke today.
Those touching words of healing,
Of what you did for me.

I know you're never far away,
I hold you close to me.
So every day I try to listen,
To hear what you have to say.

Some day's your words are loud and clear,
Yet others are soft as whispers.
Your words of love, your words of hope,
Your words of wisdom I can hear.

I never know when that time will be,
patiently you wait on me.
Until I stop and listen, LORD
To hear what you have to say.

~Linda St Myers
March 17, 2011

All references made to Joyce Meyers Magazine "Enjoying Everyday Life" May 2005 was used by permission.

Contact Information

Linda Vickery St Myers

Christian Life Purpose Coach

Pastor ~ Stephen's Minister

513-874-0514   *Lstmyers@cinci.rr.com*

www.patchworkministries.com

www.nazarene.org/ministries/women/speakers

*Sign Up for "Bits & Pieces" Daily Inspirations, Bible
Verses and Prayers through Email*

*Contributing Author to the book
"Inspired Women Succeed"
published in 2012*

Patchwork Ministry

"Putting the Pieces of Our Lives Back Together Again"

One Day Seminars Available

"Live Simply ~ Love Deeply ~ Laugh Often"
Includes "Ten Ways to Live Your Life to the   Fullest"

"It's God's Puzzle ~ not mine!"

"A Girl's Gotta Do What a Girl's Gotta Do"
Based on Esther

"Soaking in God Presence" through Prayer

"See No Evil, Hear No Evil, Speak No Evil ~ How to
Listen to God "

Other Speaking Titles – 1 Hour

Who Am I ~ Perfectly Imperfect
We are not perfect and our lives are not perfect but how do I find out "Who
I Am".

Detours of Life
When those sudden life changes come unexpectedly like an end to a
relationship, divorce, or a death of a spouse what do we do now.

Choice ~ What a Powerful Word
Are you making the right "CHOICES" in your life? How to make the right "Choices"?

"A New Season of Life" ~
Can you Rebuild and Start Over
What season are you in and can you rebuild your life ~ it's not too late to start over.

Conversations with God
When God appeared to me and what he said. How do you listen for God?

It's Okay to Feel the Way You Do
It is okay to be depressed and think everything is over but there is "Light at the End of the Tunnel".

Forgiveness~ Accepting Yourself and Taking Responsibility
You need to forgive yourself before you can forgive anyone else. Accepting that you are okay and taking responsibility for your part.

Life's a Bowl of Cherries but Why Am I Stuck in the Muck!

Small Group Discussion Teachings Available
Self-Esteem, Rejection, Boundaries
Loneliness ~Alone

Audience Testimonials

I would just like to say that Linda does a fantastic Ladies Retreat. I attended one in 2012 and the message was fantastic. She is one great lady…she made sure everything is perfect from the food and fellowship. She has a wonderful testimony and message on how she is serving God and living a Christian life. She is a blessing to know and worth the time and money to hear what she has to deliver to what God leads her to say…you won't be disappointed. ~Sandy Kuhn

Linda's seminars are wonderful, inspiring and heartfelt. She has the knowledge to speak to women in a way that makes them feel special, but she also has the life experience which lets them know she understands their situations. Linda puts the extra special touches into her seminars with real life topics, special music and gifts for each guest. You will learn a lot and laugh a lot. I highly recommend Linda's seminars and have been very blessed to have attended one myself. ~Angela Williams

If you want to be revitalized and renewed, please consider attending one of Linda's' seminars. They are fun, informative, renewing, and well worth the time. Her experience as a Life Purpose Coach and Stephen Minister adds depth to her message. She has a willing ear and a loving heart! ~Mary Melville

Linda St Myers is an excellent speaker. She is a very warm and caring person which is felt by everyone. She has a life story that every women can relate to and she shares it with humor and joy that is honoring to God. I would recommend Linda to speak for any women's group. The women will leave feeling uplifted and encouraged. ~Lynnae Bussell